PORTUGUESE
TO

A weekend's worth
of *essential* words
and phrases

Translated by
Jose and Lurdes Ferreira

First published in Great Britain in 2002 by
Michael O'Mara Books Limited
9 Lion Yard, Tremadoc Road
London SW4 7NQ

A CIP catalogue record for this book is available from the British Library

ISBN 1-85479-066-8

1 3 5 7 9 10 8 6 4 2

Designed and typeset by Design 23

Made and printed in Great Britain by William Clowes, Beccles, Suffolk

CONTENTS

INTRODUCTION

Portugal is a remarkable mix of the old and the new, and *Portuguese to go* is the ideal companion for a weekend trip to this beautiful country. Concise yet informative, a regular glance at its contents will ensure that you understand more, and are better understood. Clear and precise, the pronunciation guide that follows each word or phrase has been devised to simplify Portuguese for English-speaking users, with the aim of producing more relaxed and flowing exchanges with the people you meet.

Divided into useful, clearly marked sections, this pocket-sized language book will help the adventurous traveller to make the most of even the briefest stay in Portugal.

Diverte-te!

THE BASICS

Hello
Olá
o'lah

Goodbye
Adeus
a'de'yoosh

Good morning
Bom dia
bom dee'ah

Good afternoon
Boa tarde
boa tard

Good evening	Good night
Boa noite	**Boa noite**
boa noyt	*boa noyt*

Yes	No
Sim	**Não**
seeng	*nahng*

Please	Thank you
Por favor	**Obrigado**
pour fer'voar	*o'bree'gah'doo*

Welcome	Thank you very much
Bem-vindo	**Muito obrigado**
baim veen'doo	*mwee'too o'bree' gah'doo*

How are you?
Como está?
koo'moo esh'tah

Fine / Not bad
Bem / Assim assim
baim / ass'eem ass'eem

Pleased to meet you
Muito prazer
mwee'too prah'zair

Excuse me
Com licença
kom lee'sen'sa

Sorry
Desculpe
desh'coolp

Pardon?
Perdão?
perdahng

Do you speak English?
Fala Inglês?
fah'lah ing'lej

I don't understand
Não compreendo
nahng kom'pray'en'doo

I'm English
Sou Inglês
so ing'lej

My name is...
Meu nome é...
may'oo nom eh

Could you repeat that more slowly,
  please?
Por favor, podia repetir mais devagar?
*pour fer'voar, pood'ear re'pet'eer mysh
  de'vag'gar*

Could I pass by?
Posso passar?
poss'oo pass'ar

Why?
Porquê?
por'kay

What?
O quê?
oo kay

Who?
Quem?
kaim

When?
Quando?
kwahng'doo

How?
Como?
koo'moo

How much?
Quanto?
kwahng'too

Where?
Onde?
ond

Which?
Qual?
kwahl

How far?
A que distância?
uh kuh dish'tan'sia

Can I have...?
Posso ter...?
Poss'oo tehr

Can you tell me...?
Pode-me dizer...?
pod'muh dee'zehr

Can you help me?
Pode-me ajudar?
pod'muh ajoo'dar

GETTING FROM A TO B

AIRPORTS & ARRIVALS

Where is / where are the...?
Onde fica / onde ficam...?
ond fee'ca / ond fee'cam

baggage reclaim
a recolha de bagagem
uh re'col'ya duh bag'ah'jaim

luggage trolleys
os carrinhos de bagagem
oosh karr'een'oosh duh bag'ah'jaim

help / information desk
o balcão de informações
oo bal'kahng di een'form'as'oynsh

ladies' / gents' toilets
**a casa de banho das senhoras / dos
   homens**
*uh kaza duh ban'hgyoo duhsh
   sen'yorash / doosh ohm'aynsh*

Are there any cash machines here?
Há alguma caixa de multibanco aquí?
*ah al'gooma kysha duh mool'tee'
ban'koo akee*

Is there a bureau de change nearby?
Há alguma casa de câmbio perto?
*ah al'gooma kaza duh kamb'yoo
pair'too*

Is there a bus / train to the town centre?
**Há algum autocarro / combóio para o
centro da cidade?**
*ah al'goom ow'too'kah'roo / kom'buoyoo
parra oo sen'troo da sid'ard*

TAXI!

Is there a taxi rank nearby?
Há alguma praça de taxis perto?
ah al'gooma prah'sa duh tak'seesh pair'too

How much will it cost to get to...?
Quanto custa para ir...?
kwahng'too koosh'ta parra eer

Take me to this address please.
Leve-me a esta morada por favor.
lehvuh'muh uh esh'ta moor'ahda pour fer'voar

CAR & BICYCLE HIRE

Where can I hire a car / a bicycle?
Onde posso alugar um carro / uma bicicleta?
ond poss'oo aloo'gar oom kahr'roo / ooma bee'cee'cle'ta

I'd like to hire a car for a day / week.
Gostaria de alugar um carro por um dia / uma semana.
gosh'tar'eea duh aloo'gar oom kahr'roo pour oom dee'ah / oo'ma se'mahna

What is the daily / weekly rate?
Quanto custa por dia / semana?
*kwahn'too koosh'ta pour dee'ah /
se'mahna*

PUBLIC TRANSPORT

I'd like a single / return to...
**Queria um bilhete para / de ida e volta
para...**
*ker'eeah oom beel'yet parra / de eeda
ee volta parra*

What time does the next train / bus / tram to...leave?

A que horas é que o próximo combóio / autocarro / elétrico para...parte?

uh kuh orash eh kuh oo prohs'simoo kom'buoyoo / ow'too'kahr'oo / eel'eh'tree'koo parra ... part

Which platform do I need for a train to...?

Qual é a plataforma do combóio para...?

kwahl eh uh plata'fohr'ma doo kom'buoyoo parra

Which bus goes to...?

Qual é o autocarro que vai para...?

kwahl eh oo ow'too'kahr'roo kuh vy parra

Where should I catch the number...bus?
Onde posso apanhar o autocarro número...?
ond pohs'soo apan'yar oo ow'too'kahr'roo noom'eroo

How much is the fare to...?
Qual é o preço para...?
kwahl eh oo pray'soo parra

What time is the last bus / train / tram to...?
A que horas é o último autocarro / combóio / eléctrico para...?
uh kuh orash eh oo ool'teemoo / ow'too'kahr'roo/ eel'eh'tree'koo parra

BY SEA

Where do I catch the ferry to...?
Onde posso apanhar o barco para...?
ond pohs'soo apan'yar oo bar'koo parra

When does the next ferry / hovercraft leave for...?
Quando é o próximo barco / hovercraft para...?
kwahn'doo eh oo prohs'seemoo bar'koo / hovercraft parra

Possible responses

It's...
É...
eh

on the left / right
à esquerda / à direita
ah esh'kerda / ah deer'ayta

straight ahead
em frente
aim frent

over there
ali
alee

up / down the stairs
lá em cima / cá em baixo
lah aim see'ma / kah aim byshoo

Follow the signs.
Siga os sinais.
seega oosh see'naish

It'll cost...euros per day / per week.
Custa...euros por dia / por semana.
koosh'ta...ewr'oosh pour dee'ah / pour sem'ahna

There's a train to...at...
Há um combóio para...às ...
ah oom kom'boyoo parra...ahsh

Your train will leave from platform number...
O seu combóio parte da plataforma número...
oo sayoo kom'boyoo pahr'te duh plata'fohr'ma noom'eroo

You'll need bus number...for...
Precisa do autocarro número...para...
prais'seeza doo ow'too'kahr'roo noom'eroo...parra

The next boat for...will leave at...
O próximo barco para ... parte às...
oo prohs'seemoo bar'koo parra... pahr'te ahsh

BEDS & BREAKFAST

HOTELS & HOSTELS

Do you have any vacancies?
Tem quartos livres?
taim kwahr'toosh leev'resh

I would like...
Gostaria...
gosh'tar'eeah

I reserved a single room / double room...
Reservei um quarto de solteiro / duplo...
*rezer'vay oom kwahr'too duh sol'tayroo
/ doop'loo*

with twin beds
com duas camas separadas
kom doo'ash kah'mash separ'ah'dash

with a double bed
com cama de casal
kom kah'ma duh kazal

with shower and toilet
com duche e casa de banho
kom doosh ee kahza duh bahn'yoo

with a bath
com banheira
kom bahn'yayra

How much is...?
Quanto custa...?
kwahn'too koosh'ta

bed and breakfast...
cama e pequeno almoço...
kahma ee peek'aynoo al'moh'soo

half-board...
meia pensão...
maya pen'sahng

full-board...
pensão completa...
*pen'sahng
  kom'pleh'ta*

per night	per week
por noite	**por semana**
pour noyt	*pour sem'ahna*

I'd like to stay for...
Gostaria de ficar por...
gosh'tar'eeah duh feek'ar pour

one night / two nights
uma noite / duas noites
ooma noyt / dooash noytsh

a week / two weeks
uma semana / duas semanas
*ooma sem'ahna / dooash
  sem'ah'nash*

Is there a reduction for children?
Há desconto para crianças?
ah desh'contoo parra kree'an'sash

Do you have any cheaper rooms?
Tem quartos mais baratos?
taim kwahr'toosh mysh barr'ah'toosh

Does the room have...?
O quarto tem...?
oo kwahr'too taim

a radio / a television
um radio / uma televisão
oom rahd'yoo / ooma tele'vee'sahng

room service
serviço de quartos
sair'vee'soo duh kwahr'toosh

a mini-bar	air-conditioning
um mini bar	**ar condicionado**
oom mini bar	*ar kon'dee'sion'ahdoo*

a hairdryer
um secador de cabelo
oom sec'ador duh ka'bayloo

Is there a night-porter on duty?
Tem porteiro nocturno?
taim pour'tayoo noh'toornoo

Can I have a wake-up call at...?
Queria um seviço de despertar às...?
*ker'eeah oom sair'veesoo duh
desh'pair'tar ahsh*

I like to stay out late, so will I need a key?
**Gosto de sair até tarde, preciso de
chave para entrar?**
*gosh'too duh sa'eer ateh tard,
press'eesoo duh shahv parra entrar*

I'd like breakfast in my room tomorrow.
**Amanhã queria o pequeno almoço no
quarto.**
*amah'nyar ker'eeah oo peek'aynoo
al'mohsoo noo kwahr'too*

What time is breakfast / dinner served?
**A que horas é o pequeno almoço /
    jantar servido?**
*uh kuh oh'rash eh oo peek'aynoo
    al'moh'soo / jan'tar ser'veedoo*

The room is too cold / hot / small / dirty.
**O quarto é muito frio / quente /
    pequeno / sujo.**
*oo kwahr'too eh mwee'ntoo free'yoo /
    kaynt / peek'aynoo / soo'joo*

Could I have some clean towels please?
Queria toalhas lavadas por favor?
*ker'eeah too'al'yash lav'adash pour
    fer'voar*

The shower doesn't work.
O duche não funciona.
oo doosh nahng foon'cyon'na.

I'm not satisfied and I'd like another
  room, please.
**Não estou satisfeito e gostaria de outro
  quarto, por favor.**
*nahng esh'toe sat'ish'feitoo ee
  gosh'tar'eeah duh oht'roo kwahr'too,
  pour fer'voar*

Can you recommend any good...?
Pode recomendar alguns bons...?
pod recoom'endar al'goo'msh bomsh

BEDS & BREAKFAST

bars
bares
barsh

restaurants
restaurantes
resh'tow'ran'tesh

night clubs
night clubs
night kloo'besh

Are there any areas I should avoid at
    night?
**Há algumas áreas não recomendáveis
    para ir à noite?**
*ah al'goo'mash ahr'eeash nahng
    rec'oom'endah' vay'sh parra eer ah noyt*

34

I'd like to make a phone call.
**Gostaria de fazer uma chamada
    telefónica.**
*gosh'tar'eeah duh faz'air ooma
    sha'mahda tele'foh'neeca*

Can I have the bill?
Posso ter a minha conta?
poss'soo tehr uh meen'ya konta

CAMPING

Where is the nearest campsite?
Onde é o próximo parque de campismo?
ond eh oo pross'seemoo park duh camp'eej'moo

May we camp here?
Podemos acampar aqui?
poo'day'moosh acam'par akee

How much to stay here...?
Quanto custa ficar aqui...?
kwahn'to koosh'ta feecar akee

per day
por dia
pour deeah

per person
por pessoa
pour pessoa

per car
por carro
pour kahr'roo

per tent
por tenda
pour tenda

per caravan
por roulotte
pour rool'oht

Where are the toilets / the showers?
Onde ficam as casas de banho / os duches?
ond feecam ush kazash duh banyoo / oosh doo'shesh

Are there / is there...?
Há / há...?
ah / ah

public telephones
telefones públicos
tele'fonesh pooblee'coosh

local shops
comércio local
koomehrs'seeoo loocal

a swimming pool
uma piscina
ooma peesh'eena

an electricity supply
tomadas de corrente eléctrica
toom'ah'dash duh korr'ent eel'ect'reeca

Where's the nearest beach?
Onde fica a praia mais próxima?
ond feeca uh prya mysh pross'seema

Possible responses

We have no vacancies at the moment.
De momento estamos cheios.
*duh moo'mentoo esh'tahm'oosh
  shay'oosh*

I can recommend another hotel nearby.
Posso recomendar outro hotel próximo.
*poss'soo rec'oom'endar oht'roo ohtel
  pross'see'moo*

How long do you want to stay?
Quanto tempo tenciona ficar?
kwahng'too tem'poo tain'cee'ohna feecar

It's half-price for children.
É meio preço para crianças.
eh may'yoo pray'soo parra kree'an'sash

There are no discounts for children.
Não há desconto para crianças.
nahng ah desh'contoo parra kree'an'sash

That'll be...euros.
Serão...euros.
ser'ahng...eur'oosh

MONEY, MONEY, MONEY

GETTING IT

Where's the nearest...?
Onde fica...mais próximo?
ond fee'ca...mysh pross'seemoo

bank
o banco
oo bancoo

currency exchange office
a casa de câmbio
ah kaza duh kam'beeoo

cash machine
a caixa multibanco
ah kysha mool'tee'bankoo

What's the current exchange rate?
Qual é o câmbio do dia?
kwahl eh oo kam'beeoo doo deeah

How much commission do you charge?
Qual é a comissão a pagar?
kwahl eh uh koomees'ahng uh pagahr

I'd like to exchange these traveller's cheques / pounds for euros.
Queria trocar estes travellers cheques / libras por euros.
ker'eeah troo'cahr esh'tesh travell'ers sheh'kesh / lee'brash pour euroosh

SPENDING IT

How much is it?
Quanto custa?
kwahn'too koosh'ta

Can I pay by credit card?
Posso pagar com cartão de crédito?
*poss'soo pag'ahr kom kart'ahng duh
  kreh'deetoo*

Do you accept traveller's cheques?
Aceitam travellers cheques?
assay'tam travell'ers sheh'kesh

FOOD, GLORIOUS FOOD

EATING OUT

Waiter / Waitress!
Senhor empregado / Senhora empregada!
*sen'yor empre'gahdoo/sen'yora
  empre'gahda*

I'd like a table for one person /
  two people.
**Queria uma mesa para uma pessoa /
  duas pessoas.**
*ker'eeah ooma may'za parra oo'ma
  pessoa / dooash pess'oash*

Could we have a table...?
Podemos ter uma mesa...?
pood'ay'moosh tehr ooma may'za

  in the corner
  no canto
  noo kantoo

by the window
junto à janela
joon'too ah jan'ella

outside
lá fora
lah fohr'a

in the smoking area
na área de fumadores
nuh ahrea duh foom'ad'oresh

in the non-smoking area
na area de não fumadores
*nuh ahrea duh nahng
  foom'ad'oresh*

Could we see the drinks / food menu, please?

Podemos ter a carta de vinhos / o menu, por favor?

pood'em'oosh tehr uh kahr'ta duh veen'yoosh / oo menoo, pour fer'voar

I'd like to order some drinks, please.

Queria umas bebidas, por favor.

ker'eeah oom'ash bebee'dash pour fer'voar

I'd like ...	a bottle of...
Queria...	**uma garrafa de...**
ker'eeah...	*ooma garr'affa duh*

a glass / two glasses of...
um copo / dois copos de...
oom kohpoo / doysh koh'poosh duh

red wine
vinho tinto
veenyo teen'too

white wine
vinho branco
veenyo brancoo

sparkling mineral water
água mineral com gás
ahgwa meen'uhral kom gahj

still mineral water
água mineral sem gás
ahgwa meen'uhral sem gahj

beer	lager
cerveja	**cerveja**
sair'vayja	*sair'vayja*

cider	lemonade
cidra	**limonada**
see'dra	*lee'moon'ahda*

cola
coca cola
kohka kohla

orange juice
sumo de laranja
soo'moo duh lar'anja

apple juice
sumo de maçã
soomo duh mas'sah

Do you have a children's menu?
Tem menu de criança?
taim meh'noo duh kree'ansa

I'm a vegetarian. What do you recommend?
Sou vegetariano. O que recomenda?
so veje'tar'eeah'noo. oo quh rec'oom'endah

Does this dish contain nuts / wheat?
Este prato tem nozes / trigo?
esht prah'too taim noz'esh / tree'goo

I'd like to order...followed by...
Queria...seguido de...
ker'eeah...segee'doo duh

Could I see the dessert menu?
Posso ver o menu de sobremesa?
*poss'soo vehr oo menoo duh
  sobre'mayzah*

That was delicious. Thank you.
Estava delicioso. Obrigado.
*esh'tahva del'ees'see'ohzoo.
  o'bree'gah'doo*

Can we order some coffee, please?
Queríamos o café, por favor?
ker'eeam'oosh oo kafeh pour fer'voar

Could we have the bill, please?
Podemos ter a conta, por favor?
*pood'ay'moosh tehr uh konta, pour
  fer'voar*

Is service included?
O serviço está incluido?
oo ser'veeso eshtah een'cloo'eedoo

Do you have a complaints book?
Tem livro de reclamações?
taim oom leev'roo duh rec'lammas'yoyn'sh

Possible responses

May I take your order?
Já escolheram?
jah esh'cool'yeram

I'd recommend...
Sugiro...
sooj'eeroo

Would you like...?
Gosta...?
goshta

Enjoy your meal.
Bom apetite.
bom apet'eet'eh

SIGHTS & SOUNDS

ATTRACTIONS & DIRECTIONS

I'm lost. How do I get...?
Estou perdido. Como chego...?
eshtoe per'deedoo. koomoo shegoo

to the airport
ao aeroporto
ow air'oh'portoo

to the art gallery
à galeria de arte
ah galer'eea duh art

to the beach
à praia
ah pryya

to the bus station
à estação de camionagem
ah eshta'sahng duh cam'eeon'ajen

to the castle
ao castelo
ow cash'teloo

to the cathedral
à catedral
ah katay'dral

to the cinema
ao cinema
ow cin'aymah

to the harbour
ao porto
ow portoo

to the lake
ao lago
ow lah'goo

to the museum
ao museu
ow moo'zayoo

to the park
ao parque
ow park

to the river
ao rio
ow reeoo

to the stadium
ao estádio
ow eshtah'dee'oo

to the theatre
ao teatro
ow teeah'troo

to the tourist information office
à agência de turismo
ah ajen'cia duh toor'eejmoo

to the town centre
ao centro da cidade
ow sentroo duh sid'ahde

to the zoo
ao zoo
ow zoo

to the train station
à estação do caminho de ferro
*ah eshta'sow doo kam'eenyoo duh
  fehr'roo*

When does it open / close?
Quando abre / fecha?
kwahn'doo ahbre / fesha

Is there an entrance fee?
Paga se para entrar?
pahga'se parra entrar

Possible responses

Take the first / second / third turning on the left / right.
Vire na primeira / segunda / terceira rua à esquerda / direita.
veer nuh pree'mayra / seg'oonda / tehr'sayra rooah ah esh'kerda / dee'rayta

Go straight on.
Siga em frente.
seega aim frent

Around the corner.
Ao dobrar a esquina.
ow doob'rar uh esh'keena

Along the street / road / avenue.
siga esta rua / estrada / avenida.
*seega eshta rooah / esh'traa'dah /
aven'eedah*

Over the bridge.
Passando a ponte.
pass'andoo uh pont

It's a ten-minute walk down this road.
**São dez minutes a andar por esta
estrada.**
*sow desh meen'oot'oosh uh andar pour
eshta esh'trahda*

SPEND, SPEND, SPEND

SHOPPING

Open	Closed
Aberto	**Fechado**
ab'airtoo	*fesh'ahdoo*
Entrance	Exit
Entrada	**Saida**
entrah'da	*sy'eeda*

Where's the main shopping centre?
Onde fica o centro comercial?
ond feeca oo sentroo koom'er'seeahl

Where's the nearest...?
Onde fica o mais próximo...?
ond feeca oo mysh pross'see'moo

baker's	bank
padaria	**banco**
pah'dareea	*bancoo*

bookshop
livraria
leev'rareea

butcher's
talho
talyoo

chemist's
farmácia
far'mah'seea

clothes shop
loja de vestuário
lohja duh vesh'too'ahryoo

delicatessen
charcutaria
shar'coot'areea

department store
armazém
ar'mazaim

fishmonger's
peixaria
pay'shar'eea

gift shop
loja de prendas
lohja duh pren' dash

greengrocer's
frutaria
froot'areea

newsagent's
papelaria
puhpela'reea

post office
correios
koor'ray'oosh

shoe shop
sapataria
sapat'areea

supermarket
supermercado
soop'er'mer'kahdoo

wine merchant
casa de vinhos
kahza duh veen'yoosh

How much is it?
Quanto custa?
kwahn'too koosh'ta

Excuse me, do you sell...? aspirin
Desculpe, vende...? **aspirina**
desh'coolp, vend *ash'peer'eena*

camera films
rolos para maquina fotográfica
roll'oosh par'ra mah'kee'na
 foot'oog'rah'feeka

cigarettes
cigarros
see'gahr'roosh

condoms
preservativos
presair'va'teevoosh

English newspapers
jornais ingleses
joor'nysh een'glay'zesh

postcards
bilhetes postais
beel'yetesh poosh'tah'eesh

stamps
selos
seloosh

street maps of the local area
mapas locais
mapash look'aish

I'll take one / two / three of those...
Levo um / dois / três desses...
lehvoo oom / doy'sh / trayge dess'esh

I'll take it.
Levo isto.
lehvoo eesh'too

Where do I pay?
Onde posso pagar?
ond poss'soo pagar

That's too expensive. Do you have anything cheaper?
É muito caro. Não tem nada mais barato?
eh mween'too kah'roo. nahng taim nahda mysh barah'too

Could I have my bag, please?
Posso ter a minha mala, por favor?
poss'sooo tehr uh meenya mahla, pour fer'voar

Possible responses

Can I help you?
Posso ajuda-lo?
poss'soo aj'oodah'loo

We don't sell...
Não vendemos...
*nahng vende'
moosh*

You can pay over there.
Pode pagar ali.
pohde pagar alee

That'll be...euros, please.
São...euros, por favor.
sahng...euroosh, pour fer'voar

MEETING & GREETING

MAKING FRIENDS

Hi! My name is...
Olá chamo-me...
oh'lah shah'moo'muh

Pleased to meet you.
Prazer em conhecer-te.
prazz'air aim koon'yes'sayr'tuh

What's your name?
Como te chamas?
koomoo tuh shah'mash

Where are you from?
Donde é que és?
dondeh kuh ehsh

I'm from England.
Sou da Inglaterra.
so duh een'glat'ehrra

How are you doing?
Como vai a vida?
koomoo vy uh veeda

Fine, thanks. And you?
Bem, obrigado. E tu?
baim, o'bree'gah'doo. ee too

What job do you do?
Em que é que trabalhas?
aim kuh eh kuh trabah'lyash

Would you like a drink?
Queres uma bebida?
kair'esh ooma bebb'eeda

Two beers please.
Duas cervejas por favor.
dooash sair'vay'jash pour fer'voar

My friend is paying.
O meu amigo paga.
oo mayoo amee'goo pahga

What's your friend's name?
Como se chama o teu amigo?
koomoo suh shahma oo tayoo amee'goo

Are you single / married?
És solteiro / casado?
esh sool'tayroo / kazah'doo

Are you waiting for someone?
Estás à espera de alguém?
esh'tash ah esh'pehra duh al'gaim

Do you want to dance?
Queres dançar?
kair'esh dansar

You're a great dancer!
Danças bem!
dan'sash baim

Would you like to have dinner with me?
Queres jantar comigo?
kair'esh jantar koomee'goo

Can I have your phone number /
e-mail address?
**Posso ter o teu número de telefone /
o teu email?**
*poss'soo tehr oo tayoo noom'eroo duh
tele'fohne / oo tayoo eemail*

Here's my phone number. Call me
some time.
**Este é o meu número de telefone.
Liga-me quando quizeres.**
*esht eh oo mayoo noom'eroo duh
tele'fohne. leega'muh kwahn'doo
keez'eresh*

Can I see you again tomorrow?
Posso voltar a ver-te amanhã?
poss'soo vool'tar uh vehr'tuh ah'manyar

Possible responses

I'd love to, thanks.
Adorava, obrigado.
adoor'ahva, o'bree'gah'doo

I have a boyfriend / girlfriend back home.
**Tenho um namorado / uma namorada
na minha terra.**
*tenyoo oom nam'ooah'doo / ooma
nam'oor'ahda nuh meen'ya tehrra*

Sorry, I'm with someone. (m./f.)
Desculpe, estou acompanhado(a).
desh'coolp, eshtoe acom'pan'yahdo(a)

I've had a great evening. I'll see you
tomorrow.
**Tive uma otima tarde. Vejo-te
amanhã.**
*tee've ooma oh'teema tard.
vayjoo'tuh ah'manyar*

Leave me alone.
Deixe-me em paz.
day'she'muh aim pahsh

EMERGENCIES

Call the police.
Chame a policia.
shah'me uh pool'ees'seea

My purse / passport / car / mobile
  phone has been stolen.
**O meu porta moedas / passaporte /
carro / telemovel foi roubado.**
*oo mayoo pohrta moo'ehdash /
  passa'port / kahr'roo / teh'le'moh'vel
  foy row'bahdoo*

My wallet / bag has been stolen.
A minha carteira / mala foi roubada.
*uh meen'ya kart'ayra / mahla foy
row'bahda*

Stop thief!
Agarra que é ladrão!
agahr'ra kuh eh lad'rahng

Where is the police station?
Onde é a esquadra da policia?
*ond eh uh esh'kwah'dra duh
pool'ees'seea*

Look out!
Atenção!
Aten'sahng

Fire!
Fogo!
fo'egoo

Where is the emergency exit?
Onde está a saída de emergência?
*ond esh'tah uh sa'eeda duh
  eemer'jen'cia*

Where is the hospital?
Onde fica o hospital?
ond feeca oo oshpeet'ahl

I feel ill.
Sinto-me doente.
seen'too'muh doo'eahn'te

I'm going to be sick.
Vou ficar doente.
voe feecar doo'eahn'te

I've a terrible headache.
Tenho uma dor de cabeça terrível.
*tenyoo ooma dore duh kab'aysa
tuhr'reevel*

It hurts here...(point).
Dói'me aqui.
doh'ee'muh akee

Please call for a doctor /
an ambulance.
**Por favor chame um médico /
uma ambulância.**
*pour fer'voar shah'muh oom
meh'deecoo / ooma ambool'ancia*

I'm taking this prescription medication.
Estou a tomar estes medicamentos.
*eshtoe uh toomar eshtesh
   muh'dee'ca'main'toosh*

I'm pregnant.
Estou grávida.
eshtoe grah'veeda

I'm lost. Can you help me?
Estou perdido pode ajudar-me?
*eshtoe pair'deedoo pohde
   aj'ood'ahr'muh*

Help!
Socorro!
sook'orroo

REFERENCE

NUMBERS

0 zero
zero
zehroo

1 one
um
oom

2 two
dois
doysh

3 three
três
tresh

4 four
quatro
kwah'troo

5 five
cinco
seen'koo

6	six **seis** *saysh*	**10**	ten **dez** *dej*
7	seven **sete** *set*	**11**	eleven **onze** *onz*
8	eight **oito** *oytoo*	**12**	twelve **doze** *doa'ze*
9	nine **nove** *nov*	**13**	thirteen **treze** *trey'ze*

14 fourteen
catorze
katorz

18 eighteen
dezoito
dez'oytoo

15 fifteen
quinze
keen'ze

19 nineteen
dezanove
dez'anov

16 sixteen
dezasseis
deza'saysh

20 twenty
vinte
veent

17 seventeen
dezasete
deza'set

21 twenty-one
vinte e um
veent ee oom

30	thirty **trinta** *treenta*	**70**	seventy **setenta** *set'enta*
40	forty **quarenta** *kwar'enta*	**80**	eighty **oitenta** *oy'tenta*
50	fifty **cinquenta** *seen'cwenta*	**90**	ninety **noventa** *noo'venta*
60	sixty **sessenta** *sess'enta*	**100**	one hundred **cem** *saim*

101 one hundred and one
cento e um
sentoo ee oom

150 one hundred and fifty
cento e cinquenta
sentoo ee seen'cwenta

200 two hundred
duzentos
doo'zen'toosh

1,000   one thousand
mil
meel

5,000   five thousand
cinco mil
seen'koo meel

1,000,000   one million
um milhão
oom meel'yahng

DAYS OF THE WEEK

Monday
Segunda-feira
seg'oonda'fay'rah

Tuesday
Terça-feira
tehr'sah'fay'rah

Wednesday
Quarta-feira
kwar'tah'fay'rah

Thursday
Quinta-feira
keen'tah'fay'rah

Friday
Sexta-feira
say'shtah'fay'rah

Saturday
Sábado
sah'badoo

Sunday
Domingo
doom'een'goo

MONTHS OF THE YEAR

January
Janeiro
jan'ayroo

May
Maio
mah'yoo

February
Fevereiro
fev'er'ayroo

June
Junho
joon'yoo

March
Março
mahr'soo

July
Julho
jool'yoo

April
Abril
ab'reel

August
Agosto
agosh'too

September
Setembro
setem'broo

October
Outubro
ohtoo'broo

November
Novembro
noov'em'broo

December
Dezembro
dez'em'broo

REFERENCE

TIMES OF DAY

Today
Hoje
oarje

Afternoon
Tarde
tard

Tomorrow
Amanhã
ah'manyar

Evening
Tarde
tard

Yesterday
Ontem
on'taim

Now
Agora
agoh'ra

Morning
Manhã
manyar

Later
Mais tarde
mysh tard

TIME

Excuse me. What's the time?
Desculpe. Que horas são?
desh'coolp. kuh ohrash sahng

It's one o'clock.
É uma hora.
eh ooma ohra

It's a quarter to eight.
É um quarto para as oito.
eh oom kwahr'too parra uhsh oytoo

It's half past two.
São duas e meia.
sahng dooash ee mayah

It's a quarter past ten.
São dez e um quarto.
sahng dej ee oom kwahr'too

Five past seven.
Sete e cinco.
seht ee seen'koo

Ten past eleven.
Onze e dez.
onz ee dej

Ten to five.
Cinco menos dez.
seen'koo mennush dej

Twelve o'clock (noon / midnight)
Doze horas (meio dia / meia noite)
*doa'ze ohrash (may'yoo deear /
mayah noyt)*

Now you can order other language, ACCESS ALL AREAS and text-messaging books direct from Michael O'Mara Books Limited. All at £1.99 each including postage (UK only).

FRENCH TO GO	ISBN 1-85479-084-6
GERMAN TO GO	ISBN 1-85479-101-X
ITALIAN TO GO	ISBN 1-85479-013-7
SPANISH TO GO	ISBN 1-85479-009-9
BRITNEY SPEARS	ISBN 1-85479-790-5
CHRISTINA AGUILERA	ISBN 1-85479-780-8
CRAIG DAVID	ISBN 1-85479-948-7
EMINEM	ISBN 1-85479-793-X
S CLUB 7	ISBN 1-85479-936-3
BMX	ISBN 1-85479-145-1
HOOPZ	ISBN 1-85479-143-5
SK8	ISBN 1-85479-133-8
SNO	ISBN 1-85479-138-9
WAN2TLK? ltle bk of txt msgs	ISBN 1-85479-678-X
RUUP4IT? ltle bk of txt d8s	ISBN 1-85479-892-8
LUVTLK! ltle bk of luv txt	ISBN 1-85479-890-1
IH8U: ltle bk of txt abuse	ISBN 1-85479-832-4
URGr8! ltle bk of pwr txt	ISBN 1-85479-817-0
ltle bk of pics & tones	ISBN 1-85479-563-5
WIZTLK! ltle bk of txt spells	ISBN 1-85479-478-7
SEXTLK! ltle bk of sext!	ISBN 1-85479-487-6

All titles are available by post from:
Bookpost, PO Box 29, Douglas, Isle of Man IM99 1BQ
Telephone 01624-836000   Fax: 01624-837033
Internet: http://www.bookpost.co.uk   E-mail: bookshop@enterprise.net

Credit cards accepted.
Free postage and packing in the UK.
Overseas customers allow £1 per book (paperbacks) and £3 per book (hardbacks).